The Busy Entrepreneur: 50 Apps for Increasing Productivity, Freeing Up Your Time, and Making A Killing

Disclaimer and Terms of Use: Effort has been made to ensure that the information in this book is accurate and complete, however, the author and the publisher do not warrant the accuracy of the information, text and graphics contained within the book due to the rapidly changing nature of science, research, known and unknown facts and internet. The Author and the publisher do not hold any responsibility for errors, omissions or contrary interpretation of the subject matter herein. This book is presented solely for motivational and informational purposes only.

Table of Contents

Introduction

Right now, we're all at an age where technology is vastly and rapidly developing. One of the most prioritized is the cellular phone, try and look back to the very first phone that you owned. We have come a long way, haven't we? Nowadays, you can do almost anything with your phone and it has proved to be of great help, especially with work and other activities. But what good is a phone without any apps?

There are thousands and thousands of apps out there; apps for entertainment, fitness, studies and etc. But, we are here to talk about the practical ones, the ones that involves business and productivity. Remember when you still took down notes about every excruciating detail? When you had dozens of notebooks, paper and even sticky notes just to remind you of what you need to do? And the infuriating moment when you misplaced a crucial piece of paper? (Yes, we all have been through that moment). But now, with the use of certain apps, you don't have to go through all the hassle of having something done!

As for all things business related, all you basically need is a calculator and some paper right? But, even recording transactions in that simple manner can be hard work. It's tiring, time-consuming and quite irritating at some point. And that's not all, you won't just record theses, there's the long process of computing for the total amount. What if you don't have the time? What if it's a huge business with many transactions? Can you keep up? Fortunately, there are tons of business apps out there that are designed to make your work faster, easier, and more efficient! You might end up saying "Why did I wait so long before downloading?!" Well, you still haven't read this book, and it's about time that you start.

Now, to make your life easier and to add even more uses to your phone, we have listed the top 50 productivity and business apps that you NEED to download. Each and every one is ensured to nudge your interest and curiosity. "Can these applications do what it really states?" Yes, they can! Read each one, download and experience all the wonderful features that they offer. We're not recommending that you download all of them, just take your pick and enjoy. These are 50 of the best productivity and business apps for iPhones, you're bound to find "the one" (or maybe two) for you.

Evernote

Initially, with the word "note" in the name, you would think that it's some kind of app that takes down notes. Well, yes and no, don't get me wrong, it does takes down notes. But, this amazing all in one app also records audio, provides tags, synchronizes stored files with your other devices, and so much more! This note taking, archiving and collaboration app is one of the most widely-used productivity/business app.

Giving examples is one of the best ways to persuade, so let's say you have a newswriting job and come across a great topic like an amazing singer. Whip out that phone and create a new file on Evernote, record the singer, take a picture, add tags like "new topic" and save it. All in two minutes! When you get to your workplace, it's already synched in your desktop's Evernote. Of course, that's not all it can do.

Some great features allows users to:

- Make to-do lists.
- Access app anywhere.
- Create notebooks.
- Add or replace tags.
- Turn business cards into digital contacts.
- Save audio/images/PDF/notes.
- Organize receipts and other expenses.
- Save tickets and reservations for trips and so much more.

Another great feature is that it's available in multiple major languages. And if you go for premium, a locking feature is available where you can only access it by Touch ID or Passcode, how cool is that? Evernote saves every kind of note in every form and is accessible anytime anywhere. Oh! And the best part? It's absolutely FREE.

Dropbox

Many of you might have already heard of Dropbox, then it must be famous! May you be a busy student, a hardworking employee or even a business owner, you'll still be incredibly thankful for this app. And why is that? Well basically it's an app that lets you upload any file onto your personal online account which is accessible anywhere; just as long as you have internet connection.

Not only that, but you can immediately share any of your files with your contacts in Dropbox. A feature well appreciated by workers from different places that plan on one project; you can see their files and they can see yours. Of course you can create your own private personal folder that's separated from the others.

Its features are:

- A user friendly platform.
- 2 GB space for free accounts.
- Available in multiple major languages.
- Compatible on almost any device.
- A "favorites" option that allows you to view files offline.
- Accessible on any device with internet connection.

With Dropbox you don't have to worry about files being forgotten or misplaced, team decisions that you might have misread or even files that need to be sent to various people. And if ever (I hope it never happens) you lose your phone or your device, you can still access the files using your other devices. Worry and hassle free!

Omnifocus

Need constant reminders of what you need to do? Can't really remember what task to do next or where to go? Keep forgetting your schedule? Then, Omnifocus is here to solve your problems! Omnifocus is a powerful app that captures your plans or ideas and neatly categorizes them to cater your need.

You can put dates, places, details and names that our important to keep in mind when and what to do in your big projects, once in a lifetime occasions, and little errands or hobbies in your day to day life.

Some of its amazing features are:

- Attachment supports for files like images and audios.
- Calendar integration that enables your to work around events.
- Local notifications on deadlines.
- TextExpander Support
- Quick open which allows you to instantly go to a project, action and even folders.
- Exporting as CSV.
- Available on iPhone, iPad and Mac.
- Forecast perspective to view your actions by date.
- Sharing, Quick Entry, Location Awareness, Siri Capture and tons more.

A schedule as neatly laid out and reminded by Omnifocus ensures that there is great professional balance between your work and interest. This app will have you stay on top of your projects, you'll never experience the "oh! I forgot!" moment ever again.

Things

Have so much stuff you want to do, and yet you have no idea when and where to start? Let Things show you how it's done. With their super customizable folders and preferences, you can organize and list everything. No matter how huge the task is like preparing for a business proposal, or how small like watering the plants, even just for hobbies like being reminded to ready Pride & Prejudice, Things can organize them neatly and efficiently. All the ideas and tasks fresh from your mind goes into Things.

A few of its main features are:

- An inbox where tasks get stored if users haven't decided on a specific place yet.
- Today – where every deadline and preparation needed for the day is highlighted.
- Next – overview of all the user's upcoming tasks.
- Someday – where tasks which are not urgent are collected.
- Scheduled – shows the users all their recurring or delayed tasks.
- Projects – where tasks related to a larger task is stored.

Also, don't worry if you forget your iPhone at home because all your tasks get sent to Things Cloud. The result? You can view Things on all your Apple devices. Its platform is so easy and user-friendly, you won't need any kind of instructions at all. So plan, add, and customize according to your taste and comfort.

LogMeIn

Are you one of those people that feel the need to always bring their PC's or Macs because of some files? Even if it can be quite a hassle, some are really afraid to forget a file or something in their computer, some even feel a little paranoid if they don't. Well, LogMeIn is here to relieve you of those worries!

LogMeIn is an amazing app that gives you remote control access to your Macs, PCs and other devices. No matter where you are in the world, as long as you have internet connection and the other device is turned on, there will be no problems.

LogMeIn lets you:

- Access all the files and applications on your laptops, PCs, and other devices.
- Have your files, pictures and videos included, anywhere in the world.
- Connect with only a click of a button.
- Print files on your remote device on a local printer.
- Email files to yourself.

It's compatible with any Apple device and is available in multiple major languages. With LogMeIn, you don't have to worry of you forgot an important file or attachment and you don't have to carry around your Macs and PCs anymore. No more calling a family or friend and making them go to your house just to send you a file on a computer. No worries, no hassle.

DejaOffice

If ever you're a person who like to write notes, reminders and tasks with their contacts, it can get kind of messy and confusing with all the paper and scribbles. So we recommend DejaOffice for you. It's a powerful that holds all the users tasks, files, documents, notes, contacts, emails, meetings and CRM History. The best app to turn your iPhone into a business phone.

DejaOffice is compatible with iPhones, iPads and iPod touch. Also, DejaOffice manages contacts, calendar, tasks, memos and even expenses. It doesn't get any better than this, an app that integrates the great features of the past business apps with the advance technology today.

DejaOffice lets the users:

- Categorize the manager using colors.
- Set calendar alarms.
- Link their contacts to calendar events.
- Custom the contact fields.
- Hide their private memos.
- View summaries of daily agendas.
- Sort their contacts and so much more.
- Set advanced calendar recurrences.
- Use 3 font size which are Micro, Delightful and Business.

Also, the users can synch the following with DejaOffice:

- Microsoft Outlook
- IBM Lotus Notes
- Sage ACT!
- Palm Desktop
- Salesforce CRM
- Microsoft Outlook with Business Contact Manager

- Time & Chaos and so much more.

No more notes, no more confusion and no more mess. This all-in-one productivity app suite is bound to make your life and business management much easier.

InFocus Pro

A top app that helps you organize everything that you need to do, remember and share. From the simple things like bringing snacks at a party, to tasks in the office and everything in between. It's incredibly simple and easy to use that you're sure to finish all your projects and tasks, one step at a time.

Great features of InFocus Pro are:

- The ability to hide the user's unwanted calendars.
- Options to visually organize the user's projects using various subfolders, notes and tasks under a single view.
- Highly customizable view on the user's to do's.
- Option to customize to calendar's background with any image.
- Calendar with List, Days, Week and Month views.
- Compatible with iPhones, iPads, and iPod touch.
- Calendar that's synched with iCal, Outlook Calendar and more.

We know that most users are busy with their daily chores and tasks, and that's where another feature of InFocus Pro comes in handy. Let's say that you're driving off to work or somewhere and there's something you need to remember. InFocus Pro will speak the listed activities and assignments to you. And if you're in a hurry, you can handwrite events or to do's as a quick entry, with the choice of any color.

InFocus Pro is a powerful app that includes calendar, checklist, to do, projects and notes. One of the best ways to make your planning simpler and easier.

Google Drive

Basically, Google Drive lets the users view their files anywhere and everywhere even if their offline. Users will upload their files in Google Drive and all of it will be backed up safely and are ready to view on your iPhone, iPads and iPod touch.

When you have important files like business proposal and presentations, you can back them up for safety and easy access. You can even collaborate with workmates on documents. Once it's done, the executives and other co-workers can view, comment and edit the files in Google Drive.

Google Drive lets you:

- Immediately access any recent files.
- See all the details of any file that you uploaded.
- Enables you to view the files even when offline.
- Share files and even folders with other people in just a few clicks pf a button.
- Search for files either by their name or content.
- Set your chosen sharing permission either to view, comment or edit any file.
- View all your recent activities.

You don't have to worry of you saved the right files in your flash drive. Better yet, you don't have to chase other workers and work around their time just to get proper work done. Also, this isn't just for work, you can share all the fun adventures you had with your family and friend. All this is possible with Google Drive!

Microsoft Office

Let's face it, almost everyone uses Microsoft Office. And why not? It's very useful and now it's free in the app store plus there were tons of updates to make it easier to use. None of the "I should have bought my laptop" moment when creating new documents.

If ever you have hesitations that it won't be the same as when done on a PC, their new updates will make sure that it comes across as you hoped for. Place new ideas into Word, edit PowerPoint presentations add more values in Excel and more no matter when and where you are.

Microsoft Office app offers:

- A choice between real document layout and an easy-to-read layout.
- Features that synchronize all the editing you did on your iPhone into PC, Mac, tablets and more.
- Share your work with other by emailing them the hyperlink, PDF or the file itself.
- Easy usage of menus and navigations through touch experience.
- Automatic saving of all your files, so you don't have to worry.
- Tons of various templates.
- Tracking on changes, adding of comments and simultaneous work on the same document.
- Connection to Dropbox.
- Allows access to OneNote and OWA.

We have all used Microsoft Office at one point or another. So there's really no need for instructions and guides. Whether for work or for play, you are bound to need the Microsoft Office app.

Contactually

Nowadays, we're so busy with our work life that we lose touch with friends, co-workers and other associates. For some it might not be a reason to sound the alarm, but you should know that there are more chances and windows of opportunity open to those who have more friends and connections. But you're so busy, so how do you balance work and friendly workplace relationships?

Contactually might just be the answer to your problem. This app not only helps you organize your tasks more efficiently and reminds you of deadlines, it's also a great app that remind you to keep in touch. It shows you your last conversations with the people in your contacts and it also helps you connect with them. With just a push of a button you can talk, greet and send them a message. Slowly but surely, it will build and strengthen your relationships.

Contactually does many things for the user, like:

- Helping in managing a whole network of contacts, list of all your past interactions and notes.
- Easy access to related tasks wherever you are.
- Completing tasks, sending follow-ups, and instantly re-buckets contacts.
- Helping build better relationships with the most important people in your current network.
- Organizing your network into buckets which have automatic customizable follow-up reminders.
- Never miss out on any potential referrals ever again!

Asana

There will always come a time where we have to work or communicate with others. Having plans and projects need a lot of emails, corrections, confirmations and such. We all know how messy and confusing that is; an email from one guys, though a correction from another came too and a couple of notices for celebrations and occasions. At this rate, there's bound to be some emails that will be overlooked, but what if those are important?

That's where Asana comes in hands. It's like an online workroom, when one member posts, everyone will be able to see it. All the announcements, tasks and posts can be seen and edited, and not to mention that everyone can also post. Asana will prove to be easier and more efficient to use.

Asana's lets the users:

- Directly comment on tasks rather than emailing your teammates.
- Receive automatic status updates, related to your teams' progress on each task or projects, directly in your inbox.
- Add deadlines, followers, assignees, files and additional details into each task.
- View or organize the task list every time you open your Asana.
- Swipe right in order to immediately complete your tasks and have your teammates notified that your task is done.
- Add various tasks, projects, attachments and comments.
- Add teams up to 15 people.

No more multiple emails and various site just for communication, all you need is Asana.

Sunrise

Whenever we have tasks and occasions, we tend to put them in calendars and notes. And just like everything else, nothing is permanent so it's bound to have tons of erasures or corrections. A confusing calendar or an inefficient calendar app can really take a toll on your productivity. You would prefer a neat and easy-to-use calendar and task manager and that's what makes Sunrise one of the best calendar app.

Sunrise lets you create your own tasks and import dates, occasions and events from other calendars; Google Calendar, Facebook and more. A nice touch is the thumbnail and timeline photo imported from Facebook whenever a friend invites you to an event or if their birthday is coming up. You can also accept, decline and create events in Facebook through Sunrise.

Sunrise's amazing features are:

- Beautifully designed calendar that's 100% free.
- Smart icons and reminders.
- Time zone support that relieves you of all the headache of traveling.
- Inclusion of Facebook Events and birthdays.
- Weather forecasts which are based on your current location.
- Usage of Google Maps for directions.
- Compatible with iCloud, Exchange and Google Calendar.
- Real time synchronization.
- Able to view the faces and profiles of people you're meeting through LinkedIn.

With Sunrise, you won't ever experience that awkward "It was your birthday?!" moment. Never forget anything anymore!

Refresh

Ever had a big business meeting or interview? Remember how shy and awkward you got? Whatever can you say to the people you meet? You wouldn't want to say anything wrong or offend them, but you can't just sit there and stare all day. Impressing and making great friendly relations with executives or co-workers will attach a great record with your name. But how can you? All you need is Refresh.

Refresh is a handy app that helps you find common ground between you and the people you meet and talk to. It searches all of the available information there is about a certain person. Their accounts, personal information, hobbies, like and dislikes. Also, if you're friends on some social networking site, you can see all the posts that you're tagged to, conversations and mentions that you had. Suddenly, breaking the ice didn't seem as hard as you thought.

Its features:

- Secured personal data, it will never share any information that you input. It will always respect your privacy settings.
- Integrated with your email and even your calendar in order to keep track of all your transactions.
- Each contact will show when you first emailed, your last meeting and next meeting.
- Automatically synchs with calendar and contacts in order to automatically send insights.
- You can search for absolutely anyone, all you'll need is their name.

IFTTT

With everything that we can do with the internet and social networking sites, it's kind of hard to keep track of things. This is especially true for those who more active than others. There's so many buttons to click and sites to open just to get some tasks done. What if you want to always save pictures taken from your iPhone into Dropbox? Every time you do this, it gets a bit more boring.

So let IFTTT help you. IFTTT stands for "If This Then That", the name may be kind of confusing, but it's really easy to use. Think of it as like someone who does what you say every time. First of all, you need to create or chose something in the app called a "recipe". Example IF "I clicked favorite on a YouTube video" THEN "It will append on note". And from the time that you chose it, it will do so without fail. But, you can always turn off that option or add new ones. There might not be a task you want which IFTTT can't do.

Some of its great features:

- Tons of useful recipes to choose from or you can create your own.
- A trending page where you'll see and choose various kinds of trending recipes.
- An off switch for a recipe, in case that you don't want it to continue anymore.
- As of now, there are 140 channels available.

Workflow

Sometimes, when we have a lot of things going with our multiple accounts, we tend to waste time clicking and selecting the small options and commands just to get things done. You're a busy person and you clearly don't have time for all of that! If only there was someone who could do all of those tasks for you, someone who knew what you wanted to be done and do it without complaint.

Time to let you know, that your "someone" is Workflow. Your very own personal automated tool that enables you to create any combination of various actions in order to set your powerful workflows. From simple stuff like making files to sharing them in all of your social accounts at once. Simple, effective and faster. Also, Workflow has more than 100 actions that include ones for photos, contacts, music, Facebook, Tweeter, Dropbox, to name a few.

Actions you can do with Workflow:

- Create your very own animated GIFs
- Add home screen icons that easily calls your loved ones.
- Create PDFs from Safari or just about any app that has a share sheet.
- Get and read directions to the coffee shop nearest you with just one click.
- Tweet absolutely any song that you're currently listening to.
- Save all the images found on a web page.
- Send messages that include the last screenshot that you took and so more.

Pocket

Every day we find something interesting on the internet, but sometimes we don't have the time to fully appreciate them. May they be cute little videos, amazing images, good reads, and so on. Sometimes, we lose them and never come across them again, that's why some people pile up on the tabs. But, there's a much easier way to save these files for later.

Pocket is specially designed to save articles, images and videos in order to view later. Whenever you see something interesting, save it in pocket and be rest assured that all of them will be found in one place. It's so simple and easy to use, 12 million people have already used this app and it's time that you did too.

Some features are:

- Favorites, share and tags.
- Users can view all the files even if they are offline.
- Users can save articles, videos, webpages, recipes and more.
- Optimized viewing option for an easy-to-view layout.
- Sharing of any file on almost every social media site.
- Save as much files as you want.
- Users can change the font type to one which they prefer.
- Night mode for readers.
- Allows the users to increase or decrease the font size.
- Availability in Mac, iPhone, iPad, iPod Touch, the Web and so on.

Adobe EchoSign

Not a single person reading this has never experienced a contract or, at the very least, a need for someone's signature. Back then, whenever you need some contract agreements placed, you needed to sign it and send it. But that's not all, you also need to wait for it to get back before you can go on with your business and this can go on for weeks. It's such a hassle, expensive and can waste a lot of time.

But now, we're at the age of web contracting and Adobe EchoSign has come to our aid. This mighty useful app lets the user e-sign important documents and forms, sends them to other people whose signatures are also needed and track their responses in real time. You have an effective business contract within hours, with virtually no expense.

Adobe EchoSign's features are:

- Instantly opens and signs documents.
- Lets user directly sign the screen with their finger or stylus.
- Sign documents offline and automatically syncs them when internet connection is available.
- Sends reminders to those who have not signed yet.
- Gives copies to all the involved parties via email.
- View all the past agreements and contracts in your EchoSign account.
- Can work with documents from Dropbox, Acrobat, Google Drive and so on.

Any.do

There are so many great ways to organize all your daily, weekly and monthly tasks. But, don't you wish that it would somehow become just a tiny bit easier? Sure it's easy to write down something important, but what if you carelessly forget? Nobody want that, but it can't be helped at times.

But now we have Any.do and it's one of the best and simplest organizing app. Users can manage tons of different tasks with various people and become even more productive. It helps you organize and balance your work, home and family life. Become successful by doing one task at a time.

Any.do's features include:

- Simple design that keeps the users focused even more on their tasks.
- Collaboration with workmates, family, friends and more in order to get tasks done.
- Attach videos, audios, photos and even files from Dropbox on just about any task.
- Sets multiple recurring tasks for regularly scheduled to-dos.
- Available on iPhone, iPad and iPod Touch.
- Synchs with all your devices for easy access just about anywhere.
- Option for voice entry in order to speak the tasks into lists.
- Reminders for task's deadlines, cloud sync, customizable time and location reminders.
- Simple notes and attachments for all tasks including the shared ones.
- Easy update for all the lists and more.

Doodle

Whether you're a professional, owner of a big business or even a regular student, you have definitely experienced the pains of finding a schedule that works with those of other people. It doesn't matter if you're meeting a client, your boss or a family member, there will be conflicts in schedules. They're busy during your break and you work hard during theirs, so much time has been wasted on calls and emails just to find the perfect time between yourselves.

But with Doodle, all of those headaches and frustrations are taken away. Just send them a poll (it looks like a calendar with blank spaces and you'll indicate the time which you're available for the day) and let them choose when you will meet. It only takes about two emails and then you're done, a meeting has been set!

Doodle's features:

- Comments feature that allows the participants to communicate.
- Uses iPhone address book to invite participants.
- Optimized result view where you'll see the best times for your meetings.
- Start and track all your meeting request using your iPhone anywhere.
- Even synchronizes your calendar with other calendars like Google Calendar, Outlook, Exchange, iCal, and so on.
- Connect MyDoodle account in order to remain sync with the web dashboard.
- Easy access and even overview from your dashboard and more.

Droplr

There are tons of cool stuff on the internet and it would be cooler if you shared them with your friends and family. A shocking celebrity photo, some cute videos or babies or your very own photos. Uploading each one can be quite a hassle and it can take up space, so what can you do?

Luckily, Droplr is just the solution for your problem. It's an app that specializes in sharing photos and videos. Just upload a photo or video onto your Droplr and it will have a link that's ready to paste on any social media, email or text message. That link is ready for them to be clicked and viewed.

A few of Droplr's features:A very easy way to upload photos to share with your friends and family.

- An easy to understand streamlines workflow that's also quick to use.
- An option to view and track all those who viewed your drops.
- Account management made easier with the simple list and preview of all the user's past drop from any location.
- Shortens the links in order to share them and tracks down the number of visitors who clicked on them.
- A cloud-based application that managed all your drops and account options.

Hotel my Phone

Hotel my Phone is a really cool app that lets you "check in" to any or your friend's or family's phone. Right now, it's the first and only peer-to-peer phone sharing option. You don't have to write down important phone number in case your phone dies or you forgot your phone, no more worrying if you have enough energy in your batter to make or receive an important call. Hotel my Phone takes away all those worries.

But how does it work? Let's say you're out or you're travelling with some friends and you're waiting for an important call or text. Suddenly either your iPhone dies or your forgot to bring it with you, normally you need to go home. But now, you can use Hotel my Phone, this app will let you check in your friend's phone if they also have the app. Once you're logged in, all your messages and contacts will appear on your friend's phone. Not only that, but you can send or receive calls and texts using your number on their phone. When you log out, then all your data will also be removed from their phone. How cool is that?

App's features:

- If you're the host then the phone will switch to "hotel mode", all your personal information will be locked.
- Friend's logging out will give them 10 seconds to return the phone.
- No personal information of the user checking in will be left on the host's phone.
- If you forget to logout, it will automatically logout the account after 4 hours.

Carrot To-Do

A lot of us do things faster, or are forced to do them, when someone keeps reminding us or nag us or even make comments with double meanings. It may not be the nicest way, but things still get done anyway.

Well Carrot To-Do does actually that! It's the moody app with an attitude, kind of like your mom when she's really frustrated at you for not doing something she asked. What's great about this app is that whenever you list some tasks that you need to do and finish them you get little rewards. It's kind of like a little game and it's quite fun. But, of you don't finish your tasks, she'll get moody and you'll receive punishment like "Would you like to admit your laziness to all your social media friends?"

Carrot To-Dos features:

- Thirty six challenges to complete and they're not that easy.
- More than 500 unique and fun rewards which also varies depending on her mood.
- First four chapters is an interesting and epic branching story.
- Little fun elements like cheat codes, kitten costumes and customization options which are available through in-app purchase.
- Numerous unlockable app upgrades like reminders, mini-games and even an actual kitten and more.

You really would strive to finish your tasks if you were told something like "Hello lazy human" and "ha! That's rich." You get a reward every time you level up, and you level up by completing tasks.

Habit List

With the tons of various apps available to help you list, manage and be reminded of different daily tasks, why should you choose Habit list? There are tons of others which you might think are better than Habit List.

The things is, we always input various tasks in these applications, but what about the things that we regularly do? Do you also need to input them every time? Habit List lets you create automatic recurring lists, for example go to the gym every Monday, Wednesday and Saturday. If you accomplished them for this week, you can swipe them off and they'll still appear in next week's schedule.

Habit List's helpful features:

- Highly customizable fonts and week start date.
- Can export data and keep others private via passcode.
- Offers three schedules namely Specific Days, Non-specific Days and even Intervals.
- Instantly see your history in order to decide if your activities are working for your schedule or maybe you need to move them.
- Only shows what's due today for add more focus to the task.
- Contains colored badges that indicate where you might have slacked off and need to work on.
- Displays the remaining tasks for the day.
- Has weekly and monthly completion percentages.

ABUKAI

As a busy and productive person, you're bound to have receipts and bills that need adding, computing and categorizing to arrive at your expense report. This is fine of you have like five receipts, but what if there are dozens? It can become such a drag and waste of time, but still you need to do it. Some of us just hire others in order to get it done, but some can't afford t and others don't get the results that they wanted.

But with ABUKAI, all those problems are solved. How is that possible? Well, ABUKAI computes and categorizes everything for you, it just need a picture of the receipts. It can be done in literally just a few steps Take a picture of all the receipts, make sure it's clear, and click "Process Expense Report." In a few seconds you'll receive the complete expense report in your email alongside a PDF with the receipt's pictures. Just like magic!

Some of the amazing features are:

- Users will receive expense reports through their email in the form of Excel and PDF.
- Includes 12 expense reports per year.
- Can adapt reports to your company's own Excel format.
- Able to post the expenses into your company's expense web portal.
- App is able to directly post all the expenses into tools namely Insperity ExpensAble, Xero Accounting, Mint and Intuit QuickBooks.

PaperKarma

Our email can sometimes be filled with tons of junk email or unwanted emails. Of course you might have already found a way to get rid of it or at least minimize it. But what about your real mail? All those unwanted catalogs, subscription offers and credit card deals that are unbelievable. Those won't do any harm, but it can really be annoying to sort them out and throw them away.

But now, PaperKarma offers to stop all those annoying moments and problems. This app is dedicated into contacting the senders of the junk mail and get them to stop bothering you by sending unnecessary stuff. All you need to do is download the app, take a clear picture of the junk mail. You need to make sure that the name or the return address is captured in the photo and is visible. Once you send it to them, then they'll take care of the rest. But it make them anywhere from a few hours, to a few days or even weeks.

PaperKarma offers to:

- Track down the company sending you the junk mail and remove you from their mailing list.
- Let you track down all the mail you submitted and watch as they eliminate it.
- Help users lessen their paper waste more and more over time.

EasilyDo

Our daily lives have so much work and activities that we forget to pay attention to the little things. We don't mean to, but they sometimes slip out of our mind. For example answering emails, checking the weather, searching for ticket promos and such. Wouldn't it be nice to have someone else do it? Kind of like an assistant?

EasilyDo want to apply as your virtual assistant. It does everything you want it do to without fail. Just give out the command and you're set. There are tons of helpful commands for contacting people at designated times or getting alerts of certain people email you. You can also keep track of the weather, packages and be reminded of bills. And that' just some of what it can do.

App's amazing features:

- More than 43 automated features.
- Enter multiple reminders.
- Auto-dial to conference calls and look at the attendee's LinkedIn profiles.
- Retrieve directions and driving time to home all the way from work.
- Get the times for driving and even public transit for daily commute.
- Merge all the duplicate contacts.
- Automatically text anyone once you leave a specific location.
- Backup all your emails and attachments to Evernote, Dropbox or Box.
- View all your confirmation for movies, events, hotels and more.

TurboScan

Currently, almost everything involves some kind or word file, PDF or printed images. Though there are also a lot of instances where the files aren't in electronic form like receipts, magazine pages, books and such. You need to get a scanner in order to have a clear electronic copy. What else can you do?

Actually, there's a great portable scanner app called TurboScan. It's clear, sharp and shockingly easy to use. Maybe you're thinking that "I can just take a picture of it", of course you can, but will it be as clear? No, it won't, plus there are a handful of editing options to make the images even better. After you get the best result, you can email them to yourself in the form of multipage PDF and JPEG files.

Some it the apps features:

- Fastest processing with under 4 seconds per page.
- A mode called "SureScan" for the sharpest scans.
- Can copy pages to Clipboard.
- Adjust the size of files for a compact attachments.
- Arrange various business cards and even receipts on the PDF page.
- Instant one-tap feature for brightness, color controls and rotation.
- An "email to myself" option for instant emails.
- Automatically detects document's edge and perspective correction.
- Print through AirPrint and more.

TapWeACall

We always get a lot of important calls from various people, especially if we run a business or have an important project. Sometimes we can forget to take down notes, or we forget whatever they said. This can prove to be quite troublesome and inconvenient. Of course you wouldn't want to call them again just to ask about something that they just said, it's kind of unprofessional.

But now, with TapeACall, you can just record your conversations. It just takes a few steps, you call them then you go to the app and open it. After that, you wait for TapeACall to get ready and when it does you press merge and it will start recording. It doesn't matter if it's an incoming call or an outgoing call, it still works. And you can save and upload it almost anywhere. A great way to take down something important.

The apps features:

- No limit for the duration of the call.
- Able to record incoming and outgoing calls.
- Unlimited number of records.
- No maintenance fees whatsoever.
- Upload your record on Dropbox, Evernote, Google Drive and so on.
- Share the records through SMS, Facebook and even Twitter.
- Labels are available in order to easily search for the records and more.

1Password

We have so many stuff that we log in to, it doesn't matter if they're personal or business related. Stuff like email accounts for work and for your personal life, Dropbox, Asana, social networks and such. It's not advisable to have the same password for all of your accounts. At the end of the day, we have so many passwords that we can't even remember most of them. Of course you don't want to really write them all down, but you have no choice.

1Password is your other choice. This incredibly lifesaving app saves all your passwords into its incredibly secure vault. So when you need to log in somewhere, just click on 1Password and it will input the password for you. No more forgotten passwords ever again. It also comes with notes, folders and other personal information which are completely secured.

1Password's features:

- Able to encrypt all the data.
- Auto-lock features that secures and protects your vault if ever your device gets stolen or lost.
- Touch ID that allows instant and secure access every time.
- Synchs with all of your other iOS devices, even includes Macs and PCs.
- Wi-Fi Sync that keeps all your devices up-to-date.
- Built in browsers that can easily access and fill the logins, credit cards and identities using the Auto-fill menu.

Level Money

Since we can't all be Bill Gates, we need to track down all our income and expenses so we know how much we can spend every day. It's really hard to overspend and get debt, but it's also difficult to track and record everything. Also we tend to forget how much we spent and how much is left of our daily money or monthly income.

Good thing Level Money is there to remind, record and update us on our income, expenses and savings. We don't need to input all our expenses, Level Money connects with any of the user's bank accounts and shows how much they can spend on a daily basis. User's also input additional income that they may have or how much they want to save at the end of the month, Level Money adjusts everything accordingly. And of course, we tend to have some unpredicted expenses like plane tickets, latest gadgets or gifts, but don't worry because Level Money also considers it.

Level Money's features:

- Connects all the user's financial accounts.
- Shows how much the user can save daily, weekly and monthly.
- Users can also view their combined balance.
- View all the past transactions from bank accounts and credit cards.
- Users can connect to as many as 3,000 US-based institutions.
- Customizable notifications in order for updates on balances, credits, debits and so much more.

Suddenly, saving and spending doesn't seem to be as worrisome.

Venmo

Whoever we are and whatever we do, there will come a time when we will owe someone some money or they are the ones who owe us. It can be for business transactions, simple dinners and even rent. It can be kind of embarrassing to collect or pay money in public and sometimes you don't have any extra cash on you so you can't pay them.

With Venmo, you can pay or collect money anytime and anywhere with the use of your iPhone. You just have to connect and confirm your bank accounts and credit or debits cards before any transaction can start. Once that's done, you have the option to charge or pay money, cash out and view your account history. If you want to pay, just select a friend, put the amount and add a little note of you want. The transaction won't be complete it they don't accept the payment.

- A 256-bit encryption that secures all your information and transactions.
- User-friendly platform that can be understood by all.
- Users can share some of the transaction in their social media accounts.
- Most of Venmo's services are free of charge.
- Simple sign up instructions.
- Can accept bank deposits.

Paying and charging people doesn't feel as awkward or embarrassing as it once did, thanks to Venmo.

Mint

As you are reading this right now, we know that you have tons of account that need to be maintained, computed and looked after. Stuff like loans, insurance, income, savings, tuitions and more. How do you manage all of that? Writing them down one by one or maybe a spreadsheet? Tedious work like that can become so frustrating, but it's better than overspending and overlooking some due dates.

Mint helps the users track, categorize and compute all their earning, income and debt in order to show how much is the total and how much money is left in their bank accounts. If you have any additional earning or expenses, then you can just manually add them to arrive at the total. Also, Mint gives out reminders if something is near its due so the users can pay on time.

Mint's features include:

- Free high speed alerts.
- Option to view all the user's personal financial accounts all in one place.
- Automatically categorizes all the user's banking and credit card transactions.
- Set your own bill reminders and alerts to keep you on time.
- A free credit report summary in a matter of minutes.
- Able to set financial goals and receive great advice on how to budget and distribute all your paychecks, savings account, and more.

Quip

You find yourself at work with a lot of people which are as busy as you. You finished your part of the job and want them to look at it for some corrections, suggestion and comments. Since you really need it, you adjust your schedule to meet theirs, but they're just too busy. You end up waiting hours just for one of them, but it also happens to the other members. AT the end of the day, you're tired but the job still isn't done.

If you don't want that to happen again, then you better download Quip. One of the best apps for collaborations with co-workers. The app that seamlessly combines chat, task list, spreadsheet and docs into one. It's made to add more productivity and lessens the time taken to get jobs done. You can create and share files on iPhone, iPad and desktop with whoever you want and need.

Quip allows users to:

- Create any note, task list or documents and share them with teammates, co-workers, family and other groups.
- Chat and message in real-time with anyone.
- Import all their documents from Google Drive, Evernote, Box, Dropbox and more.
- Access all the documents from any device they use.

Quip let's work more and wait less.

Sociidot

All of us have life goals, either they are short or long term goals it doesn't really matter. Right now you might be thinking of one, how did it go? Were you successful in achieving it? Or did you lose the time, focus and will to continue? Don't worry, it happens to almost everyone and it's nothing to be ashamed of. But, wouldn't it be nice if you finally did succeed?

Sociidot is the key for finally starting and achieving all those goals of yours. It's kind of like your skillful virtual coach. This app helps you visualize your dreams and goals in the most practical way possible. Sociidot really compels you to think about your goals and your happiness. First is plotting something in the app called a "roadmap", it's basically the path that you need to follow in order to attain your goals. Once that's done, fill it with the steps you need to do in order to get to the finish line or something called "dots. You can also invite your friends to advice you every step of the way.

Sociidot's inspiring features:

- Create your own roadmap to success or edit the ones shared by others.
- Be advised by experts on the topic of your goal.
- Help say connected with people during your journey and more.

It's time to stop dreaming and start doing.

Mailbox

There are times when we look at our phone and see a dozens of text messages and missed calls. That moment can be so scary, especially if you don't know why you received so many texts and calls. You even give yourself a little pep talk before swiping that iPhone and viewing the commotion with your, already sweaty hands, only to find out that your friends just wanted to hang out. Big relief right? But, what if it was your email's inbox that was bombarded, that's even scarier. Honestly, who sends simple stuff like that in email?

So here comes Mailbox to save you from all of that. Mailbox lets you categorize your email messages into stuff to read now, later and some indefinite time. So in the end you'll just be left with the important stuff. And with frequent use, Mailbox will eventually pick up on your habit and automatically sort out the emails itself.

The app's features:

- Checks all your emails in cloud and securely sends them to your iPhone.
- Able to mute all the unimportant conversations.
- Snooze messages from your peers to this evening.
- Mainly has swipe features that's color coded and identified according to what they do.
- Able to move emails from inbox to other folders and back to inbox if the user wishes.

Before Mailbox, you would have never known that your inbox could be this clean.

Timeful

All of these calendar apps available in the stores can really help the users. They help you see what you need to do next and when or where you need to do it. Though, with all honesty, you can't really avoid skipping or nothing doing a task or two. But no matter how hard you try to hide it from everyone else or how hard you try to deny it, you have quite a number of bad habits when it comes to schedules. There's nothing wrong with that, the wrong arises if when you do nothing about it.

Using Timeful, users can view everything that they need to do and everything that grabs your attention in one place; events, occasions, meetings, chores, etc. You also include all the good habits which you want to develop. All the tasks are color-coded by level of importance. Attached to each code are the time that you need in order to finish them, where they'll take place, when and where it will happen. The app's algorithms will suggest the best times for users when they want to do certain tasks. Just the thing you need in eliminating your bad habits.

Timeful's features:

- Everything you need to do is seen on your own Calendar.
- Create schedule, to-dos and habits by just dragging them straight to the calendar.
- Categories for each of the tasks.
- Gives suggestions about the best time to do the tasks and more.

Focus@will

There are those of us who study or are more productive if we listen to music. It's calming, relaxing and it kind of separates us from our busy surroundings. Studies have showed that music can really strengthen your focus on what you are doing, it's not just myth that someone came up just because they want to listen to music. Though sometimes, it can be distracting; for example the beat is very catchy and you'll just see yourself humming and singing without a care for what your were doing before.

Luckily, Focus@will provides a great solution. What this app does is simple, it just separates the good music to the music that you shouldn't be listening to when you're trying to concentrate. It's very effective for the majority because the songs and music weren't just randomly chosen. Expert neuroscientists from UCLA a lot of effort and time in the research it took to seek out the songs that will most likely increase productivity and concentration. It's almost 100% guaranteed to work for you.

Some of this app's great features:

- Unlimited access anytime.
- No kind of credit card is needed.
- More than 10 different kinds of channels to choose from.
- Easily adjustable intensity.
- Customizable timed sessions that you can set in order to accomplish more activities.
- Listed from almost any device and more.

Newsy

If you're a person who doesn't really like to watch the news, read the paper or browse the web for discoveries, then it's time to change. There are tons of benefits which you can get from being updated about what's happening around the globe, meanwhile the benefits if you don't is absolutely none. One way or another, our personal and work lives will be affected by something in the news. Also, it can be a great topic for small talks with people and you won't be clueless every time someone brings up the latest news.

Newsy is the app that gives you videos about the latest news of the days. If you don't want to watch news videos that go on for hours at a time, then you don't need to hesitate because the videos at Newsy only offer the context and convenience of the news. In other words, they are short, bite-sized videos that won't bore you at all. It's a fun and interesting way to get updated every day.

Newsy lets the users:

- Share all the interesting and compelling new or discoveries with its simple sharing options.
- Browse and watch videos of news from all around the world through a mobile-friendly format.
- Become notified when news about particular interest and topics come out when they subscribe.

Roambi Analytics

All of us has worked or heard about some kind of "big data" or "analytics." But there are some who get confused as things get more complicated. And even fewer really fully understand what all the present data really wants to say or express. We're not all experts on the field and businesses need to explain them in layman's terms in order to captivate the audience and get a hold of their attention.

Research has stated that the best way to make people understand is by providing visuals and that's what Roambi Analytics is all about. It takes in almost any information that you provide and turns it into charts and graphs which you can highly customize. All the data is there, it's better understood and it doesn't take that much time or effort to create. Also, all the charts and graph that you create will be saved in case you need it in the future.

You can use this app to:

- Create and design various easy to use executive reports and even dashboards.
- Provide simple and understandable data to mobile workers where they need it more.
- Generate amazing experience on to data that captivate the audiences and drive adoption.
- Display all the crucial and necessary data into a single app which is 100% accessible offline. And more.

Checkmark 2

By now you have read dozens of to-do apps and may have been inclined to some of them. But, no matter how good an app is, if you can't remember what to do when you're there, then it's not that useful. It can happen to anyone, for example you reminded yourself to get milk next time you're at the grocery store. Once there, something great catches your eye, then another and another one until you get home with tons of great stuff, but no milk. It's not really a crime, but how can you change it?

Introducing Checkmark 2, a monster to-do list that works harder than others. This unbelievable app can set up reminders based on things like contacts, time and even you location. Let's have an example, let's say you set a reminder to pick up some milk and your tag two locations like Walmart and any other store on the map. Any time you're near the vicinity of any of the two apps, a reminder will pop up telling you to buy milk. How cool is that?

The app's feature includes:

- List features for projects and simple lists for entertainment.
- One-tap rescheduling.
- Location groups that allow you to attach more locations to a task.
- Highly customizable recurring reminders.
- List of sounds to choose from as a reminder tone and more.

Clear

Some people have the best of times and a lot of fun with the task managers and to-do lists that have lots of options, decorations and small simple touches. Other prefer to keep them as simple as possible and keep it as it is, just tasks, folders and a few options. If you belong with one of the former than you're bound to enjoy the above related apps. But, if you're one of the latter than it's time we introduce to you an app that you will surely like.

Clear lets you make tasks and place them in lists which you can create. This app only needs swiping and hand gestures to get things done. Swipe to one side to delete an accomplished task, swipe to the other to cross it out the list but still be able to repeat that task without creating it again. If ever you delete something important, just shake the iPhone and click undo delete. Also, you can email the list you made to yourself or just about anyone. It's so easy to use, it's very clean and simple.

Clear's features:

- Syncs to iCloud to allow access anywhere and on any device.
- Create multiple lists in order to organize your tasks further.
- One universal download for iPhone and iPad.
- Put reminders so you won't forget any tasks and so much more.

TripIt

If you're a business person who needs to travel a lot to meet clients and settle businesses or you just love travelling to other places, then you always have to plan your schedule. Planning schedules can be tiresome work, there's a lot you need to take into account and you also need to double check everything that you input especially if you're on a tight schedule. And what if you forget to put something? What if you're at the place or country and you misplace your schedule? What a total nightmare.

All of that can be avoided with TripIt. This apps just needs to get some information and emails from you and leave all the scheduling to it. Just send them a copy of your flight confirmation email, hotel booking confirmation email, and your car rental confirmation email if you have any. Once you hit send, wait a moments and it will email you back your schedule and itinerary. All your information is there alongside your earliest and latest schedule. That fast, that easy.

TripIt's key features:

- Retrieve information from your destination like directions, maps, and weather.
- Users can sync their plans in Apple Calendar, Outlook and Google Calendar.
- Manual editing and adding of plans.
- Full access to itineraries anytime and on any device.
- Share trip plan via email, social media and more.

Fantastical 2

We all need easy to understand schedules in our lives, it's also better to have more customization that are easy to control and interpret. What good are customizations if you don't know how to use it? Maybe there's something missing from all the other apps that you looked at or maybe they weren't the right app for you?

Maye Fantastical 2 is the one for you. This calendar app and task manager has so many options and features that you won't get bored when you experiment with it. But what makes this app even better, the icing on the cake if you will, is its voice command. Just say "Have lunch with Lindsey this Wednesday" and the app instantly schedules it on the calendar. Also it comes with reminders and view options so it doesn't get any better than this.

Some of the app's great features:

- Create any tasks or reminders by starting the sentences with "task" or "reminder.
- Extremely detailed map to show you the location of events.
- Birthday and TextExpander option.
- View events and reminders alongside the main list.
- Drag and drop for rescheduling.
- Search bar to look for any reminder or event.
- Tap events to view all their details and more.

Expensify

When you travel to other places you're bound to come across tons of expenses. You can't throw any receipt or any small piece of paper away, it might be important. Of course at when you get back, you might need to file an expense report, how dreadful! Repeatedly scanning receipts, writing the amounts and working your way up the total, such a pain.

But now, with Expensify, you don't need to go through all of that ever again. All you need to do is take a photo of the receipt and with a few click you can have your expense report. If you work by time, then choose the option for that and you can also track your mileage; all within the same app!

Expensify's features:

- Worldwide currency support.
- Simple and easy receipt capture.
- Available offline and on flight mode.
- Bank or credit import.
- Mobile expense creations.
- Dozens of integrations using import or export.
- Mileage entry and more.

Square Register

When you run a small business, there are tons of things that you need to settle and pay attention to. Managing various items or stocks, settling transactions, paying for fees, tracking your inventory if you have one and all that. You wouldn't really want to hire other people to do it since it's still a small business, but you might feel that it has become quite tiring on your part.

Download Square Register and turn it into you assistant. It has everything that you will ever need in growing your small business into a corporation. Square Register does everything that we mentioned above and more. Another plus is that, if you have a Square Reader or a Square Stand and live in the U.S then you can accept payment with credit cards.

Square Register's features:

- Customize all your products with phots, names and prices.
- Accepts all the major credit cards.
- Able to apply discounts and can issue refunds.
- Real time tracking on the inventory.
- Send receipts through email and text message.
- Get business insights from Square Analytics.
- Record important things like cash, gift cards and more.

AwardWallet

If you're working for a huge company, then having them send you to different cities and country is likely to happen. Of course you prepare you schedule, bring everything you need and have a checklist of what to do. It's almost always sure that you're company has enrolled you in tons of loyalty programs for car rental agencies, hotels and, of course, airlines. They may be so many that you lose track and also lose points.

AwardWallet won't ever let that happen. This app keeps track of all the loyalty programs that you are currently enrolled in. AwardWallet grants easy and fast access to any of their balances and reward number. It doesn't matter if you're online or offline, you'll still be able to see it.

Some of its major features are:

- Quick search of any loyalty program.
- A complete list of all the loyalty programs that you are enrolled in.
- Detailed view of any reward program.
- Once you are logged in, all the data is also available offline.
- Able to manage all the loyalty programs in your wallet.

Free-Time

With all the activities, chores and tasks you need to do within a day, do you still have enough free time? It may seem impossible, but there is the possibility of an hour or two if you look closely. Though some of us don't really want to know since the end results can be quite sad and unwanted. Not to be greedy or whatnot, but isn't there enough free time for yourself?

With Free-Time you can instantly see how much free time you have at the end of the day. You can also view each day of the week. It automatically searches your calendar and graphically shows you all the free time you have. You can find your availability with the push of a button. And it doesn't end there, you can also share it to friends through auto-formatted emails or text messages; it will let them know when you're free and you can meet up for some much needed unwinding.

The app's features are:

- Automatic computation and instant display of the user's free time.
- Sharing through various means like texts or emails.
- Shows when your free time and alongside the tasks that you need to do.
- Highly customizable, easy to understand and more.

Bloom*

At this point you have read a lot of apps that forces the productivity and good habit in you. What you need now is something to inspire you to create better habits and to achieve your goals. Tough love isn't a bad thing, but the feeling of being inspired to accomplish things is a totally different story.

Bloom* tend to leave you inspired to do the task that you created. The apps little ways to do it is fun, simple, creative and very unique. You can create blooms to inspire others or download those that inspired you.

What users can do:

- Create their very own unique multimedia experience from their iPhone's photo or music library.
- Download blooms that were already created in order to inspire each area of your life.
- Share any bloom with friends, family and others peers to also inspire them.
- Schedule their own alerts in order to keep focused on the things that matter and more.

Goal Streaks.

Ever wonder why it's so easy to think of a goal and start, but it's so hard to finish and achieve it? Well, maybe because most of us don't really have the best habits when it comes to achieving goals. Other reasons are that we have lost all motivation or we simple forget about it.

Goal Streaks is here to break that chain of bad habit. It only takes a few days for us to get used to a certain habit and Goal Streaks is here to help. First you create a goal and input how you can achieve it. Let's say you want to have abs so you'll go to the gym four times a week. Every time you go to the gym, click on the date and it will be marked. After a week or two you'll see the long streak in the calendar which you created. But if you miss, than you can't mark the calendar. It will show you when you broke the streak, which is encouraging since you really don't want that to happen.

The app's features:

- Users can add as much goals as they like.
- Ability to view all the goals within a single dashboard.
- Tap the day once in order to mark it done.
- Tap and hold the date to put notes and more.

Wunderlist

Basically, Wunderlist is an awesome app where you can share your to-do list with your friends, family and other peers; it helps capture your ideas and what you need to do. What makes this app so popular and so effective is that it has the right amount of features, others have too much while some have barely at all.

Wunderlist syncs into all of the user's Apple devices for a better and wider use. Users can add tasks or chores that they need to do, categorize them depending or their need and share them with your partners. It's not just an app for personal use, you and your teammates or co-workers can also share tasks needed to be done and can change the deadlines when needed. And that's just only some of what it can do.

Wunderlist's great features:

- Users are able to start conversations about their to-dos.
- Able to attach additional information like photos, PDFs, presentations and so on.
- Users can also set reminders so they won't forget any of the important tasks or deadlines ever again.
- Easy list sharing and collaboration with just about anyone and more.

Wunderlist, one of the best applications for organizing and to-dos.

Conclusion

At this point, you have read all the cool, amazing and new apps which you can download. Now, you know the secrets of some of the most successful and productive people and businesses. It's good to work hard, but it's better if you work smart. Imagine how life can be just that easier? Everything you do with your business, all the little personal activities you have and virtually anything else on your mind.

Suddenly, it's not "just" your phone anymore; it has become your business associate partner in activities and the one that tells or reminds you what to do next. It's time to start 2015 the right way, with the right apps for the job.

Think about how much awkwardness, unpreparedness, and hassle you can avoid in the future. Of course these apps weren't designed to do all the work for you, you need you give an effort too. But that small effort will go a really long way; there's only so much that an app can do.

So take that iPhone and download some, or most, of the 50 best productivity and business app for 2105. And who said that apps were only for games?